WITHDRAWN

ZOO

BY GAIL GIBBONS
ZOO

Thomas Y. Crowell
New York

Library of Congress
Cataloging-in-Publication Data
Gibbons, Gail.
   Zoo.

   Summary: Provides a behind-the-scenes
look at a working day at the zoo, from
the moment the workers arrive until the
night guard locks the gate.
   1. Zoos—Juvenile literature. [1. Zoos]
I. Title.
QL76.G46 1987   590'.74'4
87-582
ISBN 0-690-04631-6   E J590.7
ISBN 0-690-04633-2 (lib. bdg.)

Special thanks to the following people at
The Bronx Zoo, Bronx, New York:
James G. Doherty, General Curator; Dr.
Janet Stover at The Animal Health Center;
Catherine Belden, Linda Corcoran, and
David Mleczko of The Public Information
Office; Sharon Coe, keeper at The World of
Birds

It's early morning at the zoo. Here come all the workers. There's a lot to do before the visitors arrive!

Some workers sweep walkways. Others open up their souvenir stands and set out their displays.

Food vendors snap open umbrellas and put the first hot dogs on the grill.

Popcorn pops. *Sssst*…balloons fill with air.

The zoo train gets polished, and the driver tests the whistle…*toot!*

Animals from all over the world live at the zoo.

It's the zoo keepers' job to take care of them.

Each zoo keeper usually takes care of one kind of animal.

First thing every day, the keepers check on their animals. Are they safe and sound this morning?

The keepers wash down and clean out their exhibit areas. Some animals can be dangerous, so the zoo keepers must protect themselves. They will move a dangerous animal to a separate part of the cage. Once the door is locked, they can begin cleaning.

It's time for the zoo to open! The big main gates swing back, and the visitors buy their tickets.

All aboard! Visitors climb onto the train for the first tour of the day. Wheels turn, and the train pulls away from the station.

Now the zoo keepers go to their zoo kitchens. In each kitchen they prepare the special diets their animals need. Some keepers chop and mix vegetables and fruit. Others cut meat into pieces. Grain is poured, hay is stacked. Reptile keepers scoop insects into containers.

The keepers go back to their exhibit areas.

Mealtime! They feed their animals and give them fresh water.

Some animals feed themselves.

The zoo train chugs past the big-cat house. Something exciting is happening there. The zoo keepers are celebrating the birth of a baby cheetah.

Most zoo babies are born right in their exhibit areas.
The keepers and a zoo veterinarian use a TV monitor
to keep a close watch on the mother and baby.

BIRD
NURSERY

But some babies are born in special zoo nurseries.
Keepers must raise these babies until they are
big enough to go to their exhibit areas.

Crack! A baby alligator creeps out of its shell.

REPTILE
NURSERY

This exhibit is where the baby alligator
will be released when it gets bigger.
It will feel at home here.

All the zoo exhibits are designed to be like the animals' natural homes in the wild.

Lions roam over acres and acres of grassy land.

A fence and a moat keep the lions and visitors apart.

The sea lions have a pool to splash in. And they have a special feeding time. Visitors crowd around to watch them catch their food.

Monkeys swing from branch to branch in big cages.
Snakes slither over sand and wrap themselves around
logs. The snake exhibits are behind glass.

The zoo builds new exhibits from time to time.
The jungle birds are soon going to have
their own tropical forest. Pipes are installed
for a waterfall. Palm trees and ferns are planted.

This new exhibit is a zoo within a zoo. It's called the Children's Zoo. Here children can pretend to be animals. They climb the rope spiderweb and squeeze into snail shells. They pop up from gopher holes.

BE A SNAIL!

CLIMB A WEB!

There are barnyard animals to pet.
Children can feed the animals too.
A zoo keeper gives donkey-cart rides.

FEED THE CHICKS

Sometimes zoos trade animals.

The Children's Zoo traded a camel to get a new baby llama. The young llama will stay at the Children's Zoo until it is full grown.

When a zoo animal is sick or injured, the zoo must take care of it.

At the elephant exhibit the keeper has called a veterinarian to come and examine an elephant with an upset stomach. The vet gives the elephant medicine. "She'll be fine in the morning," he says.

Some animals must be taken care of at the zoo hospital.

This lion has a toothache. The vet has given him a shot so he will go to sleep. She finds the bad tooth and pulls it out.

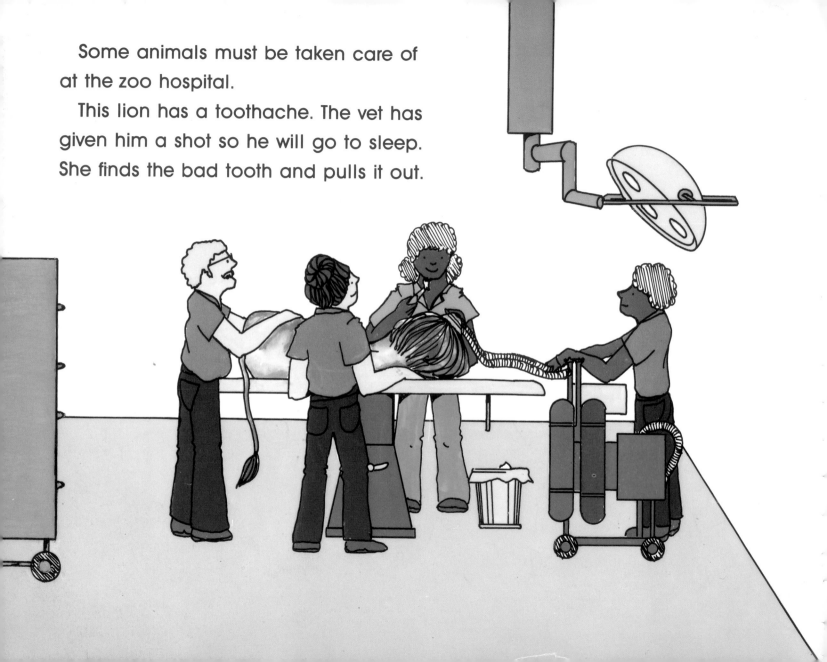

At the end of a busy day, the zoo train makes its last trip. Snack bars close, and vendors shut their umbrellas. Visitors buy last-minute souvenirs before they file out the main gates.

The gates swing closed, and a night guard locks them.

The zoo keepers check their animals one last time.

Now all the workers can go home.

A guard sets out to patrol the empty walkways.
And the animals settle down for a quiet night.

HOW ZOOS PROTECT ANIMALS OF THE WORLD

Zoos have conservation programs to protect wild animals and their natural homes.

Some animals have become scarce, because hunters have killed so many of them or because their natural homes have been destroyed. These animals are in danger of becoming extinct.
Zoos try to breed these endangered animals. When the babies are full grown, they may be kept at the zoo, or...

they may be released into their natural habitats in the wild. Zoo scientists make sure that the animals will be safe from hunters and other dangers.

Sometimes special wildlife preserves are set up to protect animals right in their natural environment.

PRESERVE